DREAM

Mark Anthony

Mark Anthony is the
bestselling poet of the
‹ soulmates › series.
He lives in the
Pacific Northwest
with his family.

Find him

on Instagram
@markanthonypoet

And Facebook
@markanthonypoet

For Bird,
my dream within a dream,
and love of my life,
and for you,
living or finding your dreams,
may this book help you
however it may.

And above all,
never give up
on the dream
of yourself.

04

Mark Anthony

Let go of your past,
it's over,
never coming back.

There is only now,
and a future
when you will look back
and see why everything
had to happen,
the way it happened,
so that you
could become
the real you.

06

Mark Anthony

Find the one
you would want
to go on
a lifelong
road trip with.

Mark Anthony

There is a love
you bring to me
with your mere presence
that is beyond words
and wisdom,
but I can tell I have it
by how soundly
I sleep with you
by my side,
and how
closely
my dreams
are to yours.

Forget what they tell you:

Do what you want.

You are your own miracle.

Your own destiny.

Your own moon and stars.

Mark Anthony

You will never have to chase
somebody who is meant
to be with you,
because they won't run.

They will stay
and stay and stay.

12

Mark Anthony

She 's a beauty,
and a badass,
and somebody
you can count on
in a storm,
so don 't take her for granted,
treat her right,
and never ever
let her go.

Mark Anthony

Love
is knowing
you're both
on the same team,
and that your dreams
and her dreams
are one and the same.

Don 't confuse romance
with roses and candy,
and pretty words by poets.

Romance is being
in the moment,
and speaking from the heart.

It 's being vulnerable to love,
and celebrating each other
as we are.

16

Mark Anthony

I don't know
what the future holds,
but I know the time
we've spent together so far
has been worth
every second.

Mark Anthony

Love will always
reveal itself
in time.

Mark Anthony

You have to love her
through her storms,
if you want her blue skies.

Mark Anthony

I fell in love with the way
I felt around her,
so innocent and alive,
I could catch the moon
between my fingers,
and eat it like ice cream.

Mark Anthony

Be brave
and feel alive;

Be human,
be love,
just be.

There is a *lunatic inside you*
wanting to write his verses to the wind,
and dance naked beneath the stars
while the earth pulses in concert
with our dreams. there is lunatic
inside of you who doesn't care
if he's poor or broken or alone
because he makes friends
with the butterflies,
and speaks the hidden
language of kings
and angels,
scribbled
in purple crayon
on bathroom stalls.

There is a *lunatic inside you*
who wants to set your heart free
to love and just be.

Mark Anthony

The truth is
we don't always end up
with the one who
we thought was the one,
but the one who came
when we were ready
to be loved
as fiercely
and deeply
as we deserve.

Mark Anthony

Sometimes
words *unspoken*
mark us
the deepest.

Mark Anthony

She 's tired of the day-to-day,
the clock, and the routine;
she wants an adventure,
and it doesn 't have
to be anything spectacular,
just a random
trip for ice cream
on a Tuesday night
where you can look
at the stars together
and remember
you 're in love.

28

In the end
we're all
looking
for someone
with the courage
to be real.

The way you wear kindness
is beautiful,
the way you feel,
the way you care,
the way you give a shit
about more than yourself
is why
I admire you,
and why
I believe
the world,
despite all of its flaws,
is still something beautiful
at heart.

I hope you fall in love
with somebody
who can see exactly
what makes you so special,
and why they are so lucky
to have you in their arms.

Never apologize
for being *yourself*.

Choose yourself.

Nobody else
can make you happy.

34

Don›t doubt,
you can do it.

You›re perfect as you are.

Time will show you,
everything you knew
deep down inside,
was true.

Mark Anthony

You deserve somebody
who will get you,
believe in you,
laugh with you,
cry with you,
sleep with you,
wake up with you,
eat with you,
walk with you,
watch a sunset with you,
listen to music with you,
talk with you,
figure it all out with you,
make mistakes with you,
forgive and forget with you,
grow with you,
and love you like there
is no tomorrow.

Mark Anthony

What if all of your fears
were really waiting for you
to overcome them,
so that you could find the courage
to be the best you
you could be.

What if every challenge
is a gift in disguise,
waiting for you to claim
another jewel
for your crown
of courage.

Mark Anthony

You are made of Stardust
and madness,
sweet honey and pearl,
and I will always love
your wild heart,
and all of your sweet
and savage ways.

Mark Anthony

The best kind of lover
is the one who isn't
in a *hurry*.

39

Bad relationships are
a dime a dozen
because so few people
know how to feel
or speak from the heart,
and it isn't until the heart
is broken that they discover
it was even there,
fragile, and rare,
and that without it,
the world loses color
and taste,
so the next time
be more careful.

Next time look deeper
inside yourself,
and listen.

40

You are not the one
who walks small,
and apologizes
for who you are.

You are the one
who knows
your own worth,
and doesn't
settle for anything less
than what
you deserve.

Mark Anthony

Listen to the warrior
inside of you,
the one telling you to
go ahead and do it,
be bold, be brave,
be the one
who steps out on a limb,
and shows the world
what you have
to offer,
without the need
for criticism or praise,
just you
being you
being you,
that's it,
that's all,
that's everything.

Mark Anthony

In the end,
there will only be a few
who really know us,
and fewer still,
will be the ones who love
what they know.

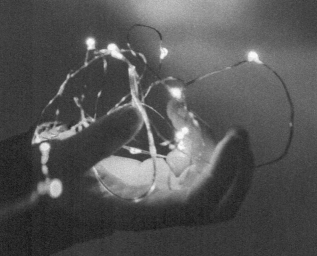

Every day she opens her heart
to the sunlight,
even when there are clouds,
even when there is rain.

She always keeps it open,
letting in whatever warmth there is,
whatever light she can get,
knowing every day is a gift
that can't be replaced,
and that the sun,
no matter how bright or dark,
is always always always there.

Mark Anthony

Find people who inspire you,
people who love your heart
and embrace your soul.

Find people who you can be yourself around,
and who pull the best out of you,
simply by loving who you really are.

Of all that I have done,
accomplished or celebrated,
there is nothing that compares
to the victory I feel
when I fall in your arms
after a long day
and know for certain
that I am home.

Follow your dreams
and forget whatever
the hell they told you
you had to be or do,
but be careful they didn't define
your dreams too
or you will be following
the wrong dreams
away from the passion
of your own heart.

Look deeply inside and ask yourself
is this what you want,
and if you get it,
how will it make you feel?

Then, go for it,
with all your heart and soul,
as if your life depended on it
because it does.

I hope you find the kind of love
that sees you, believes in you,
laughs with you, cries with you,
and holds on with you.

I hope you find a love
as fierce and forever as you deserve.

All she wants
is love,
trust,
and adventures.

I 've been to Paris
and as beautiful
as it sounds,
it wouldn 't be as beautiful
without you beside me,
holding my hand,
taking in the sky,
the buildings, the birds.

I 've seen things alone,
and even though they echo of greatness,
they are only copies of copies
of what takes my breath away,
which is your soul and my soul
standing together
somewhere in the middle of forever,
and smiling
at how lucky we are
to have found each other,
and to still be here.

Mark Anthony

She wouldn't let
others define her;
she was lovely to the bones,
and burned with a passion
that would light the night sky
and swallow the burning stars.

She wants sunlight,
and flowers,
and long walks by the sea.

She wants laughter,
and music,
and words to make her smile.

She wants all the things
that make love love
and you,
the one she's been dreaming of.

She 's tired
of being understanding
but never *understood*,
giving
but *never getting back*.

Mark Anthony

I closed my eyes
and saw you on the day we first met.
I saw the sunlight in your eyes,
and the rain in your smile,
and I knew
as surely as I know now,
so many years later,
that you were the love of my life,
and the one
I would always
adore.

I will bring you flowers
in the morning,
just for the pleasure
of seeing your smile.

I'm thinking of when we first met,
when time and space stood still,
so we could hold each other
in the back of my car,
as the moon rose above the city,
and the stars told secrets of our love.

It didn't matter
whether we were forever or a day
because some moments can nourish us
for a lifetime,
and that is how I cherish
each moment with you.

I love it when she runs her fingers
across the coastline of my body
like sheets of rain,
when the silence is ours,
and ours alone.

Mark Anthony

After heartbreak,
it's hard to want to risk love again,
but almost every love story
in the world
begins with heartbreak,
before it ends in true love.

66

I love her as she is,
doing her thing,
living her dream.

Mark Anthony

When the time is right,
you will meet somebody
who is everything you miss
from your last love,
and oh so much more.

Sometimes
you are only one choice away
from unlocking your dreams.

Make sure they recognize
the work you do,
and the heart you put in.

Even if it's not
the same kind of work
as they do,
they need to see
there is work in love,
and care,
and tenderness.

There is work
in dealing with emotions,
doing the dishes,
and fixing the lawnmower.
There is work that is
invisible to some,
but vital to others,
so make sure
they can see it,
the work you do,
and why it matters.

Mark Anthony

The fragrant flower of her skin,
the delicate murmur of her hair,
I inhale the scent of her body,
and disappear
into a wilderness of forgetting,
where the only thing left of me
is *her*.

Mark Anthony

If you ›re sad because you ›re single,
my advice to you
is to pretend as if you ›re in love.

Do all the things you would want to do,
and enjoy life to the fullest,
so that when the one
you ›re waiting for arrives,
the only thing that will change
is that you will do these things together.

Mark Anthony

74

Beauty comes from loving yourself,
and all the flaws that make you *you*.

Mark Anthony

If the world breaks your heart,
find a way to fall in love with it again.
It doesn't have to be with a person,
it could be with a poem, a peach,
or a passion, but one day
it will lead you back to the source
where nothing is lost,
and everything is forgiven.

Mark Anthony

There was a moment
when we first met,
when I could feel
our future slipping away
in the small talk,
and in the fear
of being real,
and I knew
I had to be confident
enough to be open,
honest, and vulnerable
if we were ever going
to make it past the first date.

I did,
and we did,
and I am still
proud of myself
for this brief
 moment of bravery
that turned out to be love.

Mark Anthony

I was 26
when I quit drinking,
and didn't know *how to feel*.

I was frozen inside,
and had to learn
how to feel
every emotion again,
until I wasn't afraid
to feel them.

Without this skill,
I wouldn't have been able
to find love.

I would have
made the same
mistakes as my father,
and ended up alone.

The truth is
I had to work on myself,
and heal my childhood trauma
before I could sustain
a healthy relationship,
and I think it is like that
for many men and women,
even if they don›t know it.

Mark Anthony

The world
is a better place
with *us* in it.

Mark Anthony

If you don't know whether
you miss her
or just the idea of her,
then you never really knew her.

Mark Anthony

The heart has its own *memory*,
where everything is colored with *emotion*,
and developed in time

Mark Anthony

It's possible
to have an entire relationship
where you don't really see
the other person
for who they are,
only for who
you want them to be,
and sooner or later,
the relationship will end,
and you will weep
for the love you didn't recognize
was staring you in the face
the entire time.

84

Mark Anthony

Everybody has trauma
on some level,
so you must,
as a human being,
find a way to release it,
through *therapy*,
art,
or *crying in the dark*
to some old song
on the radio.

85

Mark Anthony

An inspirational quote
means nothing
unless you find it
when you are ready
to understand the message,
and actually put it into practice.

Life is *too short*
not to appreciate its beauty.

Mark Anthony

DREAM

Sometimes
you have to imagine
the advice
you would give a friend,
as the advice
you should give to *yourself*.

90

Mark Anthony

One of life's hardest lessons
is learning that you can't save
somebody who doesn't
want to be saved,
no matter how much
you love them.

Mark Anthony

There is a reason
it's so hard
to take a *good* photograph
of the moon,
and that's because
some things
demand you respect
their mystery,
and resist
any cheap imitation,
so think of that
the next time
you take a bad selfie,
and wonder what is missing.

Mark Anthony

When you step out
of your comfort zone,
there will be chaos,
and at first you will say,
"You see this
is why I stayed
in my comfort zone",
but once you move through it,
you will be on another level
of strength and confidence,
and your new comfort zone
will be beyond
what you thought
was even *possible*
before you made that step.

Mark Anthony

One of the biggest destroyers
of a relationship,
all kinds of relationships,
is *competition*.

You should not compete
with somebody
you love.

You should support them,
and want them to succeed.

Anything less is your own
insecurity talking to the wind.

There she was,
bathing in the sunlight,
part art,
part dream,
part flesh,
bone,
and *heart*,
but all woman,
and I sat there,
thanking the universe
for such a complex
and simple beauty
as the one before me,
and knew that this life
would be nothing
but an empty shopping mall
without her.

Mark Anthony

We were never perfect,
but perfect for each other.

We fought, we fight,
we forgive, we move on.
We listen, we laugh, we cry.
We learn from each other
what love is,
and what love demands,
and that is how
you stay together
year after year.

That is how
we keep the dream alive.

Mark Anthony

There is no such thing
as being "too much"
for *the right person*.

Mark Anthony

100   There, in the quiet of your eyes,
I can see all the things I believe in.

Mark Anthony

Softly she walks
through the music
and the madness,
the moonlight
of the maze.

Her heart an open flame,
leading the way
through the darkness,
and warming
whatever is around her
with it's bright
burning passion.

Mark Anthony

Most of the time,
being in a bad mood
is a choice,
a tantrum
we throw
at the world
hoping it
will feel sorry for us,
and make
something magic happen.

Well, I've got news for you.

The magic doesn't
happen
until you quit
feeling sorry for yourself,
and move on.

In fact, that alone,
is magic.

Hey, you can do this.

You've done it before,
you will do it again.

You are never going
to give up
on the dream
of yourself.

You will keep dreaming
as long as it takes,
for your dreams
to come true.

Mark Anthony

She 's made of magic and stars,
but also rain and salt and bees;

She 's fantastic and ordinary,
flamboyant and mundane;
She 's whatever she wants to be
in the moment, and all I can do
is try to make a map of her with words
to celebrate the treasures she brings,
but the map never matches the territory,
because she is always changing,
always rearranging
into somebody deeper
than she was before,
so even as I finish this poem
it 's already too late.

Mark Anthony

Quit comparing yourself
to *others*,
when there is nothing
to find there
but unhappiness.

108

Instead,
compete with yourself
on how you can make yourself
feel the happiest.

Make your life a win-win.

Mark Anthony

Stay away from anybody
who isn't *sure* you are the one,
because their confusion
will be your heartbreak.

A *soulmate*
will never be *perfect*,
but they will be *perfect*
for *you*,
and if that doesn't make sense,
it will,
when you meet
your soulmate.

Mark Anthony

112

She's not afraid
to live her truth,
to follow her passion,
and dance to the beat
of her own heart.

Allow yourself
to *fall in love with yourself*,
and really be like,
" Damn
I am fucking awesome,
and great to hang out with,
and these people
are damn lucky
to have me in their presence
if I don 't say so myself.

Mark Anthony

Don 't forget to tell them
how much they mean to you.

It can be said over breakfast
or scribbled on a napkin
at a roadside café,
but life is short,
and it feels good to know
they know
they are loved
by you,
and even if they already do,
it doesn 't hurt for them
to hear it again.

I feel as if I've known you
since the beginning of time,
when the world was a spark,
and you were a flame,
then a fire,
then the one I love.

Mark Anthony

Don't become
hardened to life,
and love.

Heal,
and learn how
to keep your soul soft
by allowing your wisdom
to keep you safe,
and your courage
to keep you strong.

Mark Anthony

CXXIV

Her *eyes*
write poems
that leave
me speechless.

A *real relationship*
is always between two people
who are unafraid
to be vulnerable
and flawed
in front of one another,
since love shines brightest
when it is needed most.

Mark Anthony

Somebody once told me
that love is a lie,
and the feelings won't last
longer than the honeymoon,
but it's been years now,
and my feelings for her
continue to grow
stronger,
and so *never* listen
to somebody talk about love,
who doesn't know love.

We came into each other's lives
at the exact moment
when we needed each other most,
even though neither of us knew it.

Love finds you when you're ready
to recieve it.

Mark Anthony

True love
isn't such a great mystery
when you consider
every old couple,
holding hands
in the park,
probably has it,
even if to them
it's simply
love.

Mark Anthony

Life is *too short*
not to pursue
the things we love.

I'm grateful to have found a woman
who feels as deeply as the Earth,
whose fierce beauty
radiates with the stars at night,
a woman who isn't afraid to dream
of imaginary places,
a rare soul who doesn't belong
to anyone,
who is as free as the wind
on the ocean.

Mark Anthony

There is *no formula*
for attracting your soulmate
other than being a soulmate
to yourself,
until the other one
comes along.

Mark Anthony

136

Without boundaries,
there is no respect,
and without respect,
there is no true love,
no happily ever after.

Mark Anthony

Relationships
come and go,
some *happy*,
some *sad*,
some *distant*,
some *close*,
but some stay
all our lives,
and these are the ones
we call soulmates.

Sometimes there's too much work,
too much routine,
and all I want to do is crawl in bed with her,
and feel her smooth skin against mine
beneath a blanket of dreams,
as we let this messed up world go on
like an old blues record
spinning through the night
without a trace of us.

Mark Anthony

Sometimes you have to retreat,
take care of yourself,
find a place where the mind is clear,
and the heart can feel.

You have to reconnect
to yourself sometimes
before you can connect
with others,
so pay attention
to when you need space,
and know that it's not selfish,
but selfless to take it.

Find the one
who makes you wonder
how you could have ever doubted
love was real.

Mark Anthony

In order to find love,
everyone has to risk a broken heart,
because if love demands anything,
it's your heart.

Mark Anthony

It 's okay to be a dreamer
with your head in the clouds,
imagining a better world,
150   and even if the world doesn 't change,
you will,
which means the world.

We were both far from perfect when we met:
we both had scars, and bad memories,
broken dreams, and demons
that haunted us from the past,
but we saw something true in each other's eyes,
something familiar, friendly, and worth
fighting for, and so we made a promise
to each other to be real, to be honest,
to be strong, and even though
you can never know for certain
if somebody is going to stay real,
and honest, and strong, you were,
and are, and I am grateful for gambling
on your love, and winning it all.

Mark Anthony

I keep thinking the next thing
will make me happy,
the next goal, object, or idea,
and I forget I am already happy
as I am,
just being me,

so I want to write a poem
to remind me (and you)
of this truth,
so that I can smile
anytime,
anyplace,
anywhere.

Mark Anthony

Bad moods come and go
like the common cold,
so remember
they will pass,
you will get better,
and take care of yourself
in the *meantime*,
remember that you've
been here before
and it wasn't forever.

I still don't regret the time I spent
lost and searching for her,
and sometimes
when I look out at the city lights,
I imagine all the lonely strangers like me
before we met,
just so I remember
to never take her for granted,
and give thanks to the one
who filled up my lonely world
with the light of her love.

I want to wake up with you,
and hear you ask,
" What are we going to do today ? "

I want to be the one
you want to make plans with.

I want to be the one.

You deserve somebody
who is willing to do the work
it takes to stay in love.

Mark Anthony

Embrace her *heart*,
and all her *chaos*,
and *grace*,
and you will find
the *forever*
you 're looking for.

I threw myself into love and lost,
and wondered if love was even for me,
but I spent time with myself
and learned who I was,
and what I wanted
and what I did wrong,
and why love didn't work.

But how could it have
known what love was,
when i didn't even know
who I was or what I wanted.

By the time you you walked into my life,
I was already less lonely,
because I had found myself.

Love
is just a word
but your voice
is the *sound*
it makes
when it touches
my soul.

I could never live in the American dream,
with its perfection and polish.

I don't feel at home there.

I am far more comfortable in thrift shops,
and second-hand bookstores,
fast food restaurants,
and other places where the broken
and the broke congregate in the community
of the real.

So many people
dreaming of becoming millionaires,
who will never believe me when I say
all I want is enough money to pay my rent,
buy her some flowers,
and some books for myself
about other people like me
so that I know,
I am *not alone.*

166   I don't need a reason to love her,
       but I find one every time she fucking smiles.

Imagine somebody
coming into your life,
who gets your humor,
respects your ideas,
and wants all of you,
body, mind, and soul.

Mark Anthony

Real love will never make you question
if you are enough.

Mark Anthony

If you want her in your life,
act like it.

Her body would
pull me toward her
like gravity,
like the moon wanting to plunge
into the wild blue sea.

173

Mark Anthony

Poetry is a map
leading us back to ourselves.

Mark Anthony

I will remember the *laughter*.
the *kisses*, the *flames*,
the *tenderness*,
the days that all rolled together
like a joint
we smoked in bed
listening to the *endless sky*.

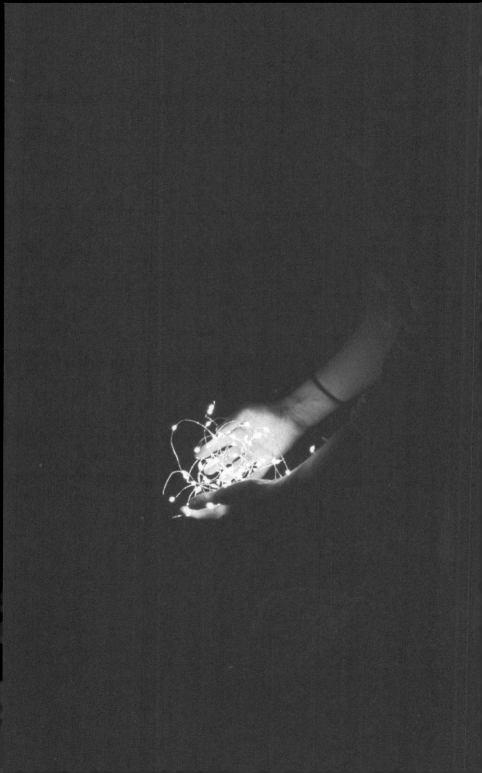

When I was only 21
and already broken by love
I had a dream I was riding on a bus,
trying to read a book,
and there was a young boy
sitting across from me,
who was really me in disguise,
and he asked if I knew
the meaning of life
and I told him,
it was to love.

I laughed at myself,
and I wondered if
I was still too young
to understand what that meant
but when it was time for the boy
to get off the bus,
I waived to him
and he was crying
the same tears
as me.

Mark Anthony

There comes a time
in every man's life
when his books of philosophy
no longer matter,
and he has to face
the long night alone,
without anybody's theories
to keep him warm,
and he will know why
love will always be
greater than knowledge.

180

Mark Anthony

182

Some people
never question
why
they do what they do,
so it's no surprise
they are
sad
for reasons
they can't explain.

Mark Anthony

We found a low-rent apartment
on the outside of town and filled it
with flowers and candles,
and books about Paris,
and promised each other
one day we'd save enough to go,
but you can't save much
on minimum wage,
so we bought some wine
and bread and broke it
and imagined it was Paris,
as we made love to the sound
of French music
and laughed
at what fools
we were,
but we were *happy*,
and knew that Paris
could be anywhere.

Learn to love the moments
between destinations,
the quiet moments with yourself,
the slow moments when life
seems to be waiting to give you
your next instruction;
trust that you're preparing
for the next stage of your life,
and be ready when the next door opens,
and it's time to walk inside.

Mark Anthony

I get lost in the wild of your eyes.
I dream, I fall among the flowers
and the breezes,
until the world awakes me again.

I have to wrestle time with one hand
and my love with the other,
day after day,
just so I can catch another glimpse
of the wild in your eyes
that keeps me dreaming and alive.

Mark Anthony

I had to destroy
who I thought I was
in order to discover
who I am.

Front cover by Adryan RA
Back cover by Altınay Dinç

Audiobook by
Michael Hajiantonis
Instagram @michael.hajiantonis,
www.michaelhaj.co.uk

Designed & Edited by
Elias Joseph Mennealy
Benjamin Browning

photography 8

Alecsander Alves
Jessica Felicio
Micah hill
Dexter Fernandes
Natalya Letunova
Marcus Wallis
Javardh
Zoltan Tasi
Natalya Letunova
Rhett Wesley
Chance Monnette
Altinay Dinc
Benjamin Wedemeyer
Alecsander Alves
Mohamed Nohassi
Tom Barrett
JoelValve
Luigi Colonna
Clay Banks
Josh Boot
Biel Morro
Sebastián León Prado
Icarius
mohsen ameri
Bruce Christianson
Adryan RA
Jamie Street
Rohan Makhecha
Jon Ly
Yeshi Kangrang

Mohamed Nohassi
Dawid Zawila
Mark Rabe
Jamie Street
Josh Boot
Sanni Sahil
Sasha Freemind
Alejandro Tocornal
Julián Cárdenas
Adryan RA
Jamie Street
Rohan Makhecha
Jon Ly
Yeshi Kangrang
Mohamed Nohassi
Dawid Zawila
Mark Rabe
Jamie Street
Josh Boot
Ben Koorengevel
Chinh Le Duc
Dev Benjamin
Do Kwon
Geraldine Li
Julián Cárdenas
Guilherme Stecanella
Aziz Acharki
Brynden

DREAM

Mark Anthony

DREAM
by Mark Anthony Poet

Published by Vagabond
www.vagabond.ltd
5455 Wilshire Boulevard,
Los Angeles, CA 90036

MARK ANTHONY POET
Instagram @markanthonypoet
facebook.com/markanthonypoet

PRODUCT ID: 4835234902

FIRST EDITION

13 12 11 10 9 8 7 6 5 4 3 2 1

Visit ID.VAGABOND.LTD and enter your
product ID for a free audiobook and full
color ebook download.

194

Mark Anthony

DREAM

198

Mark Anthony